Resolving Property Disputes in Indian Families

C. P. Kumar
Reiki Healer
Roorkee - 247667, India

Disclaimer

While every effort has been made to ensure the accuracy and completeness of the content in this book, the author cannot guarantee that the information contained herein is error-free, up-to-date, or suitable for every individual circumstance.

The author shall not be held liable or responsible for any errors or omissions in the content of the book, nor for any damages, or losses that may arise from any actions taken based upon the suggestions or contents presented in the book.

Readers are advised to use their own judgment and discretion in applying the information provided in this book, and to consult with qualified professionals before taking any action based on the contents of this book. The author disclaims any and all liability or responsibility for any actions taken or not taken based on the information contained in this book.

DEDICATION

This book is dedicated to all the families who have experienced the turmoil and challenges of property disputes. You have faced the complexities and emotional strains that arise when disputes arise within the sacred bonds of kinship. Through this dedication, I express my gratitude for your unwavering support and love, which has fueled my determination to shed light on this crucial topic.

Chapter by chapter, we embark on a journey together, exploring the intricacies of property disputes within Indian families. From understanding the cultural context that shapes these conflicts to navigating the legal framework and exploring alternative methods of resolution, this book seeks to empower families with knowledge and strategies to find peaceful resolutions.

To my dear readers, I extend my heartfelt appreciation for your curiosity and interest in this critical subject matter. It is my sincerest hope that the insights shared within these pages will provide you with valuable guidance, enabling you to approach property disputes with empathy, wisdom, and fairness.

May this book serve as a beacon of knowledge and a source of inspiration to all those who are entangled in property disputes, fostering understanding and harmony within Indian families. Together, let us build a future where conflicts are resolved with compassion and foresight, ensuring the preservation of family bonds and the legacy of unity.

C. P. Kumar

CONTENTS

PREFACE

Resolving property disputes within families is a multifaceted endeavor that requires a delicate balance of legal understanding, cultural context, and emotional intelligence. In the Indian subcontinent, where familial ties and the concept of shared heritage hold great significance, these disputes can often become deeply entrenched, causing rifts that span generations. It is within this complex landscape that the need for guidance and knowledge becomes paramount.

This book, "Resolving Property Disputes in Indian Families," aims to provide a comprehensive resource for individuals and families facing the challenges of property disputes. It delves into the intricate tapestry of Indian society, exploring the cultural factors that influence such conflicts and the unique legal framework governing property rights and inheritance. By examining the various types of property, from ancestral to self-acquired and joint, we aim to clarify the distinctions and shed light on their significance in dispute resolution.

Each chapter offers valuable insights and practical strategies for navigating the intricate web of property disputes. From the importance of accurate documentation and evidence to the role of family elders in providing wisdom and guidance, we explore the diverse tools available for finding equitable solutions. Additionally, we delve into the processes of partition and division, negotiation techniques, and the role of mediation and arbitration in facilitating peaceful resolutions. We also examine alternative dispute resolution methods, the role of courts, and the legal remedies that can be pursued.

Beyond the legal and procedural aspects, we recognize the emotional impact that property disputes can have on families. The book addresses the deep-rooted emotions and family dynamics involved, aiming to foster empathy and understanding among all parties. Furthermore, we emphasize the significance of future planning, offering proactive measures to prevent property disputes and promote harmonious family relationships.

It is our sincere hope that this book serves as a guiding light for individuals, families, and professionals involved in property disputes. By equipping readers with knowledge, strategies, and a compassionate approach, we aspire to contribute to the resolution of conflicts and the preservation of familial bonds. Our ultimate goal is to empower readers to navigate property disputes in a manner that upholds fairness, respect, and the enduring values of Indian families.

As you embark on this journey through the chapters, we encourage you to approach the content with an open mind, ready to absorb the insights and apply them in your unique circumstances. May this book serve as a beacon of guidance, fostering harmony, and resolution within Indian families facing property disputes.

C. P. Kumar
Reiki Healer
Former Scientist 'G', National Institute of Hydrology
Roorkee - 247667, India
E-mail: cpkumar@yahoo.com
Web: https://www.angelfire.com/nh/cpkumar/virgo.html

Chapter 1. Introduction to Property Disputes

Understanding the complexity of property disputes within families

Property disputes within families can be emotionally and financially challenging, often leading to strained relationships and legal battles. In the context of Indian families, property disputes hold a particular significance due to cultural and societal norms surrounding property ownership, inheritance, and family dynamics. This introductory chapter sets the stage for understanding the complexity of property disputes within Indian families and highlights the need for effective resolution strategies.

Importance of Property Dispute Resolution: Property disputes have far-reaching implications, impacting not only the individuals involved but also the overall well-being of the family unit. These disputes can result from conflicting interpretations of property ownership, inheritance laws, changing family dynamics, or financial considerations. Resolving property disputes in a fair and amicable manner is crucial to preserve family harmony and ensure a secure future for all family members.

Emotional Toll of Property Disputes: Property disputes often evoke intense emotions and can strain relationships among family members. The attachment to family property, the sense of entitlement, and the fear of losing valuable assets can intensify the emotional impact. Understanding and addressing the emotional aspects of property disputes are essential for fostering open communication, empathy, and effective resolution.

Cultural and Societal Factors: Property disputes in Indian families are influenced by cultural and societal factors deeply rooted in traditions, customs, and inheritance laws. The concept of ancestral property, joint family structures, and cultural expectations surrounding property division further complicate the dynamics of property disputes. Exploring these cultural factors helps in understanding the unique challenges and sensitivities associated with resolving property disputes in an Indian context.

Legal Framework: Property disputes are governed by a complex legal framework that varies based on regional laws, personal laws, and inheritance laws in India. Familiarity with relevant laws, such as the Hindu Succession Act, the Indian Succession Act, and state-specific regulations, is crucial for understanding property rights, inheritance principles, and the legal remedies available to resolve disputes.

Complexity of Property Ownership: Differentiating between ancestral property, self-acquired property, and joint property adds to the complexity of property disputes. Ancestral property holds special significance in Indian families, and its division requires careful consideration of legal and cultural aspects. Understanding the different types of property and the rights associated with them lays the foundation for addressing property disputes effectively.

Impact of Changing Family Dynamics: Changing family dynamics, such as the transition from joint families to nuclear families, can impact property disputes. The shift in family structures, individual aspirations, and economic independence may give rise to conflicting expectations and disputes over property rights. Recognizing and adapting to these changing dynamics is essential for finding sustainable resolutions.

Importance of Documentation and Evidence: Maintaining accurate documentation and evidence is crucial in property dispute resolution. Proper documentation includes property titles, ownership records, inheritance documents, and transaction records. The availability of credible evidence strengthens legal claims, facilitates objective decision-making, and minimizes disputes arising from conflicting interpretations.

Role of Mediation and Alternative Dispute Resolution: Mediation and alternative dispute resolution methods play a significant role in resolving property disputes within families. Mediation provides a neutral and facilitated platform for open communication, active listening, and collaborative problem-solving. By engaging in dialogue and negotiation, families can explore mutually beneficial solutions and avoid the adversarial nature of litigation.

Importance of Legal Remedies: Understanding the legal options available for resolving property disputes is essential for informed decision-making. Legal remedies such as partition, division, injunctions, and specific performance can be explored depending on the specific circumstances of the dispute. Being aware of these legal avenues empowers families to navigate the legal process effectively.

Long-Term Implications: Property disputes can have long-term implications on family relationships, financial stability, and overall well-being. Timely resolution of property disputes minimizes financial and emotional costs, prevents prolonged legal battles, and ensures a secure future for all family members. By addressing property disputes proactively, families can preserve their unity and create a foundation for future harmony.

In conclusion, property disputes within Indian families are complex and require a comprehensive understanding of legal, emotional, and cultural aspects. This introductory chapter provides an overview of the challenges associated with property disputes and sets the stage for the subsequent chapters of the book, which delve deeper into specific topics and strategies for resolving property disputes in Indian families. By recognizing the complexity of property disputes and adopting proactive resolution approaches, families can navigate these challenges and achieve amicable outcomes while preserving family relationships and ensuring a secure future for all.

Chapter 2. Cultural Context

Exploring the cultural factors influencing property disputes in Indian families

The resolution of property disputes within Indian families is deeply intertwined with the cultural fabric of the country. India, with its diverse cultural heritage and rich traditions, presents a complex landscape where cultural factors play a significant role in shaping the dynamics and outcomes of these disputes. To effectively navigate property disputes in Indian families, it is essential to delve into the cultural context and explore the intricate interplay of customs, traditions, societal norms, and family dynamics that influence these conflicts.

One of the key cultural factors that influence property disputes in Indian families is the strong emphasis on ancestral property. Ancestral property holds immense significance as it represents a shared heritage and legacy passed down through generations. The concept of joint ownership and the expectation of preserving ancestral wealth for future generations can often create tensions and conflicts when it comes to property division. The cultural belief that ancestral property should remain within the family and be managed collectively can contribute to complex disputes, particularly in joint family setups.

In addition to ancestral property, the cultural norms surrounding inheritance play a pivotal role in property disputes. India has a diverse array of personal laws based on religion, such as Hindu, Muslim, Christian, and others, which influence the principles of inheritance and succession. These laws often have varying rules and interpretations regarding the distribution of assets among heirs. Cultural expectations, obligations, and traditions regarding the division of property further add complexity to the resolution process. In some cases, cultural practices may prioritize the interests of male heirs or favor certain family members based on traditional gender roles or hierarchical structures.

The influence of family dynamics and hierarchies is another crucial aspect of the cultural context in property disputes. Indian families are typically characterized by strong family ties, respect for elders, and a collective decision-making process. Family structures often revolve around patriarchal authority and the joint decision-making of senior family members. These dynamics can impact the resolution of property disputes, as power imbalances, conflicting interests, and the weight of family expectations can complicate negotiations and create challenges in finding a fair and equitable solution.

Social and societal pressures also exert an influence on property disputes within Indian families. The desire to maintain social standing, preserve family honor, and uphold the reputation of the family can significantly impact the resolution process. Societal norms and expectations regarding property ownership, inheritance, and wealth distribution can shape the motivations and actions of individuals involved in property disputes. Fear of judgment, stigma, or ostracization may influence decision-making and create additional barriers to effective resolution.

Religion and religious customs also play a significant role in shaping property disputes within Indian families. Different religious practices and beliefs influence concepts of ownership, inheritance, and the distribution of assets. Religious rituals and traditions associated with property division can hold deep cultural significance and impact the decision-making process. Understanding the religious and cultural nuances specific to each family and religion is essential for resolving property disputes in a manner that respects and aligns with their beliefs and values.

Effective resolution of property disputes in Indian families necessitates a nuanced understanding of the cultural factors at play. It requires embracing cultural sensitivity, empathy, and a deep appreciation for the diverse perspectives and traditions that shape familial relationships. Recognizing and respecting the cultural context can contribute to fostering dialogue, building trust, and finding mutually acceptable resolutions.

To navigate property disputes successfully, it is crucial to promote open communication and dialogue among the parties involved. Encouraging transparent discussions about cultural expectations, beliefs, and concerns can help bridge gaps in understanding and identify common ground. By fostering an environment that values respect, empathy, and cultural sensitivity, individuals and families can work towards finding solutions that are acceptable and sustainable within their cultural context.

Professional mediators and legal experts handling property disputes in Indian families should also possess a deep understanding of the cultural nuances and traditions that influence these conflicts. They should be equipped with the knowledge and skills to navigate culturally sensitive issues, facilitate effective communication, and bridge cultural gaps. Mediation processes that incorporate cultural sensitivity can provide a conducive platform for open dialogue, enabling parties to explore creative solutions that respect their cultural values while addressing their underlying interests.

In conclusion, the cultural context plays a significant role in shaping property disputes within Indian families. Ancestral property, inheritance principles, family dynamics, societal pressures, religious customs, and social norms all contribute to the complexity of these conflicts. By exploring and understanding the cultural factors at play, individuals and professionals involved in property dispute resolution can approach the process with cultural sensitivity, empathy, and a deeper appreciation for the diverse perspectives and values that shape these disputes. By doing so, we can foster dialogue, preserve family harmony, and achieve fair and equitable resolutions that are respectful of the cultural context within which these disputes arise.

Chapter 3. Types of Property

Differentiating between ancestral property, self-acquired property, and joint property

In the context of property disputes within Indian families, understanding the different types of property is paramount. Property disputes often arise due to conflicting interpretations of ownership rights, entitlements, and obligations associated with various types of assets. Ancestral property, self-acquired property, and joint property are three distinct categories that require careful differentiation to navigate property disputes effectively. In this chapter, we delve into the intricacies of these property types, examining their legal implications, cultural significance, and the role they play in resolving property disputes within Indian families.

Ancestral property holds a significant place in the Indian legal and cultural landscape. It refers to property that is inherited through generations, passed down from one generation to the next. The key characteristic of ancestral property is its uninterrupted lineage of ownership, usually in joint ownership among family members. The legal framework governing ancestral property varies depending on personal laws, religious customs, and regional practices. In some cases, ancestral property may be subject to specific legal provisions that protect the rights of all family members and restrict the sale or partition of such property. Understanding the concept of ancestral property is crucial for determining the rights and entitlements of family members during property disputes, as it forms the bedrock of shared heritage and inheritance within Indian families.

Self-acquired property, as the name suggests, refers to assets that an individual acquires through their own efforts or inheritance. Unlike ancestral property, self-acquired property is not subject to joint ownership but is owned solely by the individual who acquired it. This type of property can include land, buildings, financial assets, businesses, or any other form of tangible or intangible assets. Self-acquired property is often governed by the laws of succession and personal preferences of the individual owner. During property disputes, the ownership and distribution of self-acquired property are typically determined based on legal principles, testamentary documents such as wills, or the rules of intestate succession when no valid will exists. Clarifying the status of self-acquired property is essential in resolving disputes, as it distinguishes individual ownership rights from the collective ownership associated with ancestral property.

Joint property refers to assets that are owned collectively by multiple individuals, often within the same family. Joint property can include both ancestral and self-acquired property that is intentionally held in joint ownership by family members. This type of property is governed by specific legal provisions and can present unique challenges during property disputes. Joint property can be subject to shared responsibilities, decision-making, and potential conflicts arising from differing interests or contributions. The resolution of disputes related to joint property requires a careful analysis of the ownership shares, contributions made by each party, and the legal rights and obligations associated with joint ownership. Understanding the nuances of joint property is crucial for finding equitable solutions and preserving family harmony.

Differentiating between these types of property is pivotal in resolving property disputes within Indian families. The determination of property type forms the foundation for understanding ownership rights, legal entitlements, and the distribution of assets among family members. During property disputes, clarifying the nature of the property in question enables the application of relevant legal principles, the assessment of individual and collective interests, and the exploration of possible resolutions.

Navigating property disputes involving ancestral property requires an examination of the legal framework, including the provisions of personal laws, religious customs, and regional practices. It is crucial to identify and interpret relevant legal precedents, court judgments, and legal provisions specific to ancestral property. These considerations help establish the rights and obligations of family members and provide a basis for negotiation, mediation, or legal proceedings aimed at resolving disputes.

Resolving disputes related to self-acquired property necessitates a comprehensive understanding of testamentary documents, such as wills, and the principles of succession applicable to the particular religious or legal framework. Careful examination of the legal validity, authenticity, and interpretation of such documents is crucial in determining the rightful ownership and distribution of self-acquired property. Disputes regarding self-acquired property may require probate proceedings, estate administration, or court interventions to ensure a fair resolution.

Addressing property disputes involving joint property entails a meticulous examination of ownership agreements, joint tenancy, or other legal instruments governing the joint ownership. Understanding the contributions, intentions, and agreements made by each party involved in the joint ownership is vital for finding equitable solutions. Resolving disputes related to joint property often requires negotiation, mediation, or legal proceedings focused on identifying the fair distribution of assets, clarifying ownership shares, or seeking partition or division of the property.

Moreover, cultural and emotional aspects are intertwined with property disputes involving all three types of property. Cultural factors, such as the perception of collective ownership, family expectations, and traditional practices, significantly influence the dynamics of property disputes within Indian families. Emotional considerations, such as the attachment to ancestral property or the sense of entitlement to self-acquired property, can add complexity to the resolution process. Recognizing and addressing these cultural and emotional dimensions is crucial for fostering understanding, empathy, and facilitating effective communication among family members during property disputes.

In conclusion, differentiating between ancestral property, self-acquired property, and joint property is essential in resolving property disputes within Indian families. Each type of property carries distinct legal implications, cultural significance, and ownership dynamics. Understanding the nuances of these property types provides a foundation for navigating the complexities of property disputes, determining ownership rights, and finding equitable resolutions. By comprehending the legal, cultural, and emotional aspects associated with each property type, individuals and families can approach property disputes with clarity, sensitivity, and a greater likelihood of achieving fair and harmonious outcomes.

Chapter 4. Understanding Inheritance

Discussing the principles of inheritance and succession in the Indian subcontinent

In the Indian subcontinent, the principles of inheritance and succession play a significant role in shaping property rights, family dynamics, and, consequently, property disputes within families. Inheritance laws and practices in India are complex and diverse, influenced by religious, cultural, and legal frameworks. Understanding the intricacies of inheritance is essential for individuals and families involved in property disputes, as it forms the basis for determining the rightful heirs, their entitlements, and the distribution of assets. In this chapter, we delve into the principles of inheritance in the Indian subcontinent, exploring the various religious and legal perspectives, the role of personal laws, and their implications for resolving property disputes within Indian families.

The principles of inheritance in the Indian subcontinent are deeply rooted in religious beliefs and customs. Different religions, such as Hinduism, Islam, Christianity, Sikhism, and others, have distinct laws and practices governing inheritance. Each religion has its own set of religious texts, scriptures, and interpretations that guide the principles of inheritance. These religious perspectives often form the basis for personal laws that apply to individuals adhering to specific religious faiths.

In Hinduism, the concept of ancestral property and joint family systems significantly influence inheritance practices. The Hindu Succession Act of 1956 governs the inheritance and succession of property for Hindus, Buddhists, Jains, and Sikhs. The Act underwent significant amendments in recent years to promote gender equality and remove gender-based biases in inheritance. The amended Act grants daughters equal rights to ancestral property, challenging the traditional notion of male primogeniture.

Islamic law, known as Sharia, guides inheritance practices for Muslims in the Indian subcontinent. Under Sharia, specific shares are allocated to different family members, such as spouses, children, parents, and siblings. The distribution of inheritance in Islam is based on fixed proportions, ensuring the fair and just distribution of assets among heirs. Understanding the principles of Islamic inheritance is crucial for resolving property disputes involving Muslim families, as it provides a framework for determining the entitlements of heirs and the distribution of assets.

Christian inheritance law in India is governed by various personal laws, depending on the denomination and affiliation of the individual. Christian inheritance practices are influenced by canon law and specific provisions within personal laws applicable to different Christian communities. The principles of testamentary succession, intestate succession, and the rights of heirs are determined based on these personal laws.

In addition to religious laws, the legal framework in the Indian subcontinent also plays a significant role in inheritance and succession. The Indian Succession Act of 1925 provides a general framework for testamentary and intestate succession applicable to individuals irrespective of their religious affiliation. This Act applies to individuals who do not fall under the purview of specific personal laws. The Act addresses various aspects of inheritance, including wills, probate, administration of estates, and the determination of heirs.

Navigating property disputes related to inheritance requires a deep understanding of the relevant personal laws, religious texts, and legal provisions. The interpretation and application of these laws depend on specific circumstances, family structures, and the intentions of the deceased individual. In cases where a valid will exists, the document guides the distribution of assets according to the wishes of the deceased. However, in the absence of a will, the laws of intestate succession come into play, determining the entitlements of family members based on predefined legal principles.

Resolving property disputes involving inheritance often requires a delicate balance between legal considerations, cultural norms, and familial expectations. The inheritance laws and practices in the Indian subcontinent are influenced by deeply ingrained cultural traditions and social dynamics. The cultural expectation of preserving family wealth, maintaining collective ownership, and respecting the wishes of the deceased can add layers of complexity to property disputes. Disputes may arise due to differing interpretations of religious texts, conflicting claims from heirs, or challenges to the validity of testamentary documents.

Mediation and negotiation play crucial roles in resolving property disputes related to inheritance. Mediation allows conflicting parties to engage in facilitated discussions, promoting understanding, empathy, and the exploration of mutually agreeable solutions. Mediators with a deep understanding of the cultural and legal aspects of inheritance can provide a conducive environment for open dialogue and help bridge gaps between family members. Negotiation techniques that focus on preserving relationships, respecting cultural sensitivities, and finding compromises can contribute to successful outcomes in inheritance-related property disputes.

Legal interventions, such as probate proceedings, can also be necessary in cases where the validity of wills is contested, or when disputes cannot be resolved through negotiation or mediation. Court interventions provide a formal and authoritative resolution to property disputes, applying the relevant personal laws and legal provisions to determine the rightful heirs and the distribution of assets.

It is crucial for individuals and families to seek legal advice from experts specializing in inheritance laws and property disputes to navigate the complexities of inheritance effectively. Understanding the religious, cultural, and legal nuances associated with inheritance is essential for making informed decisions, asserting rightful claims, and ensuring a fair resolution to property disputes.

In conclusion, understanding the principles of inheritance and succession in the Indian subcontinent is vital for resolving property disputes within families. Religious, cultural, and legal factors significantly influence inheritance practices, shaping ownership rights, entitlements, and the distribution of assets. By exploring the religious and legal perspectives, navigating personal laws, and recognizing the cultural nuances, individuals and families can approach property disputes related to inheritance with a greater understanding, empathy, and the potential for finding equitable resolutions.

Chapter 5. Legal Framework

Overview of the legal system and relevant laws governing property disputes in the Indian subcontinent

The resolution of property disputes in Indian families is deeply intertwined with the legal framework that governs property rights, ownership, and inheritance. A comprehensive understanding of the legal system and the relevant laws is essential for effectively navigating property disputes and seeking fair and just resolutions. In this chapter, we provide an overview of the legal framework in the Indian subcontinent, exploring the key legislations, court systems, and legal principles that influence property disputes within Indian families.

The legal system in the Indian subcontinent is a complex web of laws influenced by various factors, including historical precedents, colonial legacies, religious practices, and regional customs. The Constitution of India forms the cornerstone of the legal system, providing the fundamental rights and principles that guide the administration of justice. The Constitution establishes a federal structure, with a central government and individual state governments having jurisdiction over different matters, including property laws.

Property laws in India are primarily governed by the Transfer of Property Act, 1882, which outlines the general principles of property ownership, transfers, and rights. This Act provides a legal framework for the acquisition, transfer, and disposal of property, including provisions on leases, mortgages, and gifts. The Act also addresses the concept of joint ownership and co-ownership, which are crucial aspects in property disputes involving multiple stakeholders within a family.

In addition to the Transfer of Property Act, personal laws based on religious practices and customs govern property disputes within specific religious communities. These personal laws differ depending on the religious affiliation of individuals and include the Hindu Succession Act, Muslim Personal Law, Christian Personal Law, and others. These personal laws outline the principles of inheritance, succession, and property rights applicable to individuals adhering to specific religious faiths.

The Hindu Succession Act of 1956 is particularly significant in property disputes within Hindu families. The Act governs inheritance and succession for Hindus, Buddhists, Jains, and Sikhs. It underwent significant amendments in recent years to promote gender equality, ensuring that daughters have equal rights to ancestral property. These amendments challenge the traditional notion of male primogeniture and enable women to assert their rightful claims in property disputes.

Muslim personal law, based on the principles of Sharia, governs property disputes among Muslims in the Indian subcontinent. The principles of Islamic inheritance, as outlined in Sharia, provide specific guidelines for the distribution of assets among heirs. Sharia emphasizes fairness and just distribution, ensuring that specific shares are allocated to different family members based on their relationship to the deceased. Understanding the principles of Islamic inheritance is crucial for resolving property disputes involving Muslim families.

The legal system in the Indian subcontinent is supported by a hierarchical structure of courts that adjudicate property disputes and other legal matters. The courts include district courts, high courts, and the Supreme Court of India. District courts serve as the primary trial courts and handle civil disputes at the district level. High courts have appellate jurisdiction, hearing appeals from lower courts and addressing complex legal issues. The Supreme Court, the highest judicial body in India, serves as the final appellate authority and also has the power of judicial review.

Alternative dispute resolution methods, such as mediation and arbitration, also play a significant role in resolving property disputes within Indian families. Mediation provides a platform for facilitated discussions, enabling parties to explore mutually agreeable solutions and reach a settlement with the assistance of a neutral mediator. Arbitration involves the submission of disputes to an arbitrator or a panel of arbitrators, who make a binding decision based on the evidence and arguments presented by the parties. These alternative methods offer a more flexible and less adversarial approach to dispute resolution, allowing for greater control and participation by the disputing parties.

When property disputes cannot be resolved through negotiation, mediation, or arbitration, litigation becomes necessary. Litigation involves the formal resolution of disputes through the courts, with each party presenting their arguments and evidence before a judge. Litigation can be a lengthy and costly process, but it provides a definitive legal resolution and ensures adherence to the principles of justice and fairness.

To effectively navigate property disputes within the legal framework of the Indian subcontinent, individuals and families are advised to seek legal advice from professionals specializing in property laws and dispute resolution. Legal experts can provide guidance on the specific laws and regulations applicable to a particular case, offer insights into court processes and procedures, and help individuals assert their rights and entitlements. Legal representation ensures that the interests of individuals involved in property disputes are adequately protected and advocated for in the legal arena.

In conclusion, understanding the legal framework governing property disputes is crucial for effectively resolving conflicts within Indian families. The legal system in the Indian subcontinent encompasses various legislations, personal laws, and court systems that influence property rights, ownership, and inheritance. By familiarizing themselves with the relevant laws and seeking appropriate legal advice, individuals and families can navigate property disputes more effectively, assert their rights, and seek fair and just resolutions. Additionally, alternative dispute resolution methods can provide a more flexible and collaborative approach to resolving property disputes, while litigation offers a formal and binding resolution when necessary.

Chapter 6. Documentation and Evidence

Importance of maintaining accurate records and evidence in property disputes

Property disputes within Indian families can be complex and emotionally charged, often revolving around conflicting claims, disputed ownership, or contested entitlements. In such contentious situations, the role of documentation and evidence becomes paramount. Maintaining accurate records and gathering supporting evidence is crucial for establishing ownership rights, validating claims, and presenting a strong case during property disputes. In this chapter, we delve into the importance of documentation and evidence, exploring the types of records, their significance, and the practical steps individuals can take to ensure a strong evidentiary foundation in property disputes within Indian families.

Accurate and comprehensive documentation serves as the backbone of property ownership and provides crucial evidence to substantiate claims. It is essential to maintain records that establish the chain of ownership, the mode of acquisition, and any subsequent transactions related to the property. This includes deeds, sale agreements, wills, gift deeds, mortgage documents, lease agreements, and any other legal instruments associated with the property. Properly executed and registered documents carry legal weight and can serve as vital evidence in property disputes.

Ancestral property, in particular, requires diligent record-keeping and documentation. Ancestral property records should establish the lineage of ownership, trace the origins of the property, and record any subsequent transactions or partitions. It is advisable to maintain records of inheritance, partition deeds, family settlements, and any other relevant documents that reflect the collective ownership and transfer of ancestral property over generations. Accurate and updated genealogical records can also be useful in establishing rightful claims and ownership shares.

In addition to property-specific documentation, it is crucial to maintain records that establish possession, usage, and improvements made to the property. These records can include utility bills, property tax receipts, maintenance invoices, photographs, and any other supporting evidence that demonstrates active possession and investment in the property. Such evidence can be instrumental in establishing a long-standing connection to the property and countering claims of adverse possession or abandonment.

Financial records also play a significant role in property disputes. It is advisable to maintain records of financial transactions related to the property, such as purchase receipts, payment receipts, bank statements, loan agreements, and property-related expenses. These records can help establish the financial investment made in the property, the sources of funding, and the contributions made by individuals involved in the dispute.

Furthermore, documentary evidence can extend beyond property-specific records. Correspondence, letters, emails, and other forms of communication that discuss or reference the property can be valuable evidence. Such records can demonstrate the intent, understanding, and agreements between parties involved in the property dispute. It is important to preserve any written communication related to the property, especially those that may clarify ownership, obligations, or intentions.

To ensure the integrity and admissibility of the documentation and evidence, it is crucial to adhere to proper record-keeping practices. This includes maintaining originals or certified copies of documents, organizing them systematically, and keeping them in a secure location. It is advisable to make digital copies or scans of important documents as a backup measure. Maintaining a well-organized and accessible record of all relevant documents can streamline the process of gathering evidence and strengthen the legal case during property disputes.

Apart from documentation, gathering supporting evidence is equally important. Evidence can include witness testimonies, expert opinions, photographs, site surveys, property appraisals, and any other relevant material that supports the claims or disputes. It is essential to gather evidence promptly and ensure its authenticity and relevance to the dispute. In some cases, it may be necessary to engage professionals, such as surveyors, appraisers, or forensic experts, to provide objective assessments and opinions on property-related matters.

The admissibility and weight of evidence in property disputes are determined by legal principles and court procedures. It is essential to familiarize oneself with the rules of evidence and procedures specific to property disputes in the Indian legal system. Engaging legal experts specializing in property law can provide valuable guidance on the types of evidence required, the admissibility of different forms of evidence, and the strategies for presenting a strong case.

In property disputes within Indian families, emotions and personal relationships can complicate the resolution process. Documentation and evidence provide an objective foundation that can help steer the focus towards factual aspects and legal principles. They serve as a common ground for parties to assess their respective claims objectively and negotiate or mediate based on verifiable facts. Well-maintained records and strong supporting evidence can facilitate constructive discussions, foster clarity, and contribute to the resolution of property disputes in a fair and just manner.

In conclusion, maintaining accurate documentation and gathering supporting evidence is of utmost importance in property disputes within Indian families. Proper record-keeping establishes ownership, traces the history of the property, and substantiates claims, while evidence provides additional support and validation. By ensuring diligent record-keeping practices, organizing relevant documents, and gathering objective evidence, individuals can build a strong evidentiary foundation for their claims and contribute to the resolution of property disputes based on factual and legal grounds.

Chapter 7. Navigating Joint Family Property

Strategies for handling property disputes in joint family setups

Property disputes within joint family setups present unique challenges due to the complex dynamics and shared ownership that characterize such arrangements. In Indian families, where the joint family system has deep cultural roots, property disputes can often become emotionally charged and contentious. Navigating these disputes requires a nuanced understanding of the intricacies of joint family property and the adoption of specific strategies aimed at fostering communication, preserving relationships, and seeking fair resolutions. In this chapter, we explore strategies for effectively handling property disputes in joint family setups, taking into account the legal, cultural, and emotional aspects that come into play.

Open Communication: Establishing open lines of communication among family members is crucial in addressing property disputes. Encouraging respectful dialogue and providing a platform for all stakeholders to express their concerns, perspectives, and expectations can foster understanding and empathy. Active listening and effective communication techniques, such as paraphrasing and summarizing, can help ensure that everyone feels heard and acknowledged.

Mediation and Facilitation: Engaging a neutral third party, such as a mediator or family facilitator, can facilitate constructive conversations and help parties explore mutually acceptable solutions. Mediators are trained professionals who can guide discussions, manage conflicts, and encourage collaborative decision-making. They can provide a safe and structured environment for family members to express their interests, identify common goals, and work towards resolving the property dispute.

Clarifying Ownership and Rights: Clearly defining ownership shares, rights, and responsibilities of family members regarding the joint family property is essential. Creating an agreement or legal document that outlines the distribution of shares, rules for usage, and decision-making processes can help prevent disputes and establish a transparent framework for managing the property. Seeking legal advice to draft such documents can ensure clarity and enforceability.

Regular Family Meetings: Conducting regular family meetings provides a forum for discussing property-related matters and addressing any emerging conflicts proactively. These meetings can serve as a platform to review the status of the property, address concerns, and make joint decisions regarding maintenance, improvements, or future plans. The meetings should be inclusive, allowing all family members to participate and contribute to the discussions.

Professional Property Management: In some cases, engaging a professional property manager or administrator can help alleviate disputes by taking over the day-to-day management and maintenance responsibilities. A property manager can provide objective oversight, handle financial matters, maintain records, and ensure equitable usage of the property. This approach can remove biases and personal interests from property-related decisions.

Partition and Division: In situations where disputes cannot be resolved amicably, partitioning or dividing the joint family property may be a viable option. Partition refers to the division of the property into separate shares for individual family members. The process may involve physical division or the allocation of shares based on appraised value. Seeking legal assistance during partition ensures compliance with legal requirements and the equitable distribution of assets.

Seeking Expert Advice: Consulting legal professionals and experts specializing in property disputes can provide valuable guidance throughout the resolution process. Legal experts can offer insights into relevant laws, assess ownership rights, and help navigate complex legal procedures. Expert opinions from professionals such as appraisers, surveyors, or financial advisors can contribute to the valuation and division of property in a fair and transparent manner.

Preserving Relationships: It is crucial to prioritize the preservation of family relationships throughout the resolution process. Property disputes have the potential to strain relationships, but fostering empathy, respect, and understanding can help mitigate conflicts. Encouraging family members to maintain open lines of communication, expressing appreciation for shared heritage, and focusing on long-term family bonds can create a more conducive environment for resolving property disputes.

Considering Alternative Dispute Resolution: Exploring alternative methods of dispute resolution, such as arbitration or family settlement, can provide a more flexible and confidential approach. Arbitration involves submitting the dispute to an arbitrator or a panel of arbitrators who make a binding decision based on evidence and arguments. Family settlements involve reaching a mutually agreed-upon resolution with the assistance of legal advisors. These methods can offer faster and more tailored solutions than traditional court litigation.

Adhering to Legal Processes: When disputes cannot be resolved through negotiation or alternative methods, seeking legal recourse may be necessary. Understanding the legal processes, timelines, and requirements for property disputes is essential. Engaging competent legal representation can help protect individual rights, advocate for fair resolutions, and ensure compliance with applicable laws.

Preserving Documentary Evidence: Maintaining accurate records and preserving relevant documentary evidence is crucial in joint family property disputes. Records should include property-related documents, financial transactions, agreements, and any other evidence that supports claims or ownership rights. Well-organized and easily accessible records contribute to building a strong case and provide clarity during the resolution process.

Empathy and Understanding: Recognizing the emotional aspects involved in property disputes within joint family setups is essential. Empathy, understanding, and sensitivity towards the concerns and perspectives of other family members can foster an environment of mutual respect and cooperation. Acknowledging the shared history, traditions, and cultural significance of the joint family property can help create a shared sense of responsibility and facilitate fair resolutions.

Resolving property disputes within joint family setups requires a delicate balance between legal considerations, cultural sensitivities, and familial relationships. By adopting strategies that prioritize open communication, mediation, clarifying ownership rights, and seeking professional advice, individuals can navigate the complexities of joint family property disputes with greater success. Preserving relationships, prioritizing fairness, and understanding the emotional impact of property disputes contribute to a more harmonious resolution process and ensure the preservation of familial bonds.

In conclusion, navigating property disputes in joint family setups requires a multifaceted approach that encompasses legal, cultural, and emotional considerations. Strategies such as open communication, mediation, clarifying ownership, and seeking expert advice provide a framework for resolving disputes effectively. By adopting these strategies, individuals can promote understanding, preserve relationships, and seek fair resolutions in property disputes within Indian families.

Chapter 8. Role of Family Elders

Utilizing the wisdom and guidance of family elders in resolving disputes

Within the context of Indian families, the role of family elders holds significant importance in resolving property disputes. Family elders, often revered for their wisdom, life experience, and knowledge of cultural traditions, can play a crucial role in facilitating communication, providing guidance, and fostering harmony within the family. Their involvement in the resolution of property disputes brings a sense of authority, respect, and cultural understanding that can contribute to the successful resolution of conflicts. In this chapter, we explore the role of family elders in resolving property disputes in Indian families, emphasizing the value of their wisdom and guidance.

Cultural Significance of Family Elders: In Indian society, family elders hold a revered position due to their age, life experiences, and accumulated wisdom. They are seen as repositories of cultural values, traditions, and ethical principles. Respecting the authority and guidance of family elders is deeply ingrained in Indian culture and plays a vital role in maintaining family harmony. Leveraging their cultural significance can create an environment conducive to resolving property disputes.

Mediators and Peacemakers: Family elders often serve as mediators and peacemakers in property disputes. Their impartiality, neutrality, and long-standing relationships with family members make them well-suited to facilitate constructive dialogue and negotiations. Their role as mediators can help bridge communication gaps, bring conflicting parties together, and foster understanding and empathy among family members.

Historical Knowledge and Context: Family elders possess valuable historical knowledge and context that can shed light on the origins and evolution of family property. They can provide insights into the intentions of previous generations, clarify traditional practices, and explain the cultural significance of the property. Their knowledge helps establish the historical and cultural context necessary for resolving property disputes.

Moral Authority: Family elders often have moral authority within the family, commanding respect and trust from younger generations. Their involvement in the resolution of property disputes can lend credibility and influence in guiding family members towards fair and just outcomes. Their moral authority can help in shaping decisions, encouraging compromises, and ensuring adherence to cultural values and ethical principles.

Cultural Traditions and Customary Practices: Family elders are well-versed in cultural traditions and customary practices that govern property rights and inheritance in Indian families. They can provide guidance on the interpretation of religious texts, customs, and rituals associated with property disputes. By explaining the cultural norms and values, family elders can help resolve conflicts while respecting the family's heritage and traditions.

Facilitating Family Meetings: Family elders can play a pivotal role in convening and leading family meetings dedicated to resolving property disputes. By chairing these meetings, they ensure that all family members have an opportunity to express their concerns, listen to differing perspectives, and collectively work towards a consensus. Family elders' presence can set a tone of respect, patience, and empathy during these meetings.

Mentorship and Wisdom: Family elders can act as mentors, offering guidance and imparting wisdom gained from their life experiences. They can counsel younger family members involved in property disputes, helping them understand the broader implications, long-term consequences, and ethical considerations associated with these disputes. Their mentorship can guide family members towards making informed decisions and finding amicable solutions.

Resolving Conflicts through Storytelling: Storytelling is an age-old tradition in Indian culture, used to impart wisdom, moral lessons, and historical context. Family elders can employ storytelling techniques to illustrate the significance of the property, convey lessons from past disputes, and inspire family members to find common ground. Storytelling can create empathy, foster understanding, and encourage collaboration in resolving property disputes.

Balancing Interests and Fairness: Family elders can provide an objective perspective by considering the interests of all family members involved in the dispute. They can help balance the desire to preserve family unity with the need for fair distribution and resolution. Their guidance can contribute to finding equitable solutions that consider individual needs, family dynamics, and the long-term sustainability of family relationships.

Preserving Family Legacy: Family elders have a vested interest in preserving the family's legacy and heritage. They understand the importance of maintaining familial bonds, passing down values, and sustaining the unity of the family across generations. By actively participating in property dispute resolutions, family elders contribute to preserving the family's legacy and fostering a sense of cohesion.

Facilitating Compromises and Mutual Understanding: Family elders possess the ability to foster compromises and mutual understanding among family members. They can help individuals recognize shared interests, common goals, and the importance of preserving family relationships. Through their guidance, family elders encourage family members to prioritize resolution over personal gain and work towards outcomes that benefit the collective well-being.

Seeking Collaborative Solutions: Family elders promote collaboration rather than adversarial approaches to dispute resolution. They encourage family members to engage in constructive dialogue, explore alternative options, and find win-win solutions. By emphasizing cooperation and mutual respect, family elders contribute to resolving property disputes in a manner that maintains family harmony.

It is important to note that while family elders play a crucial role in resolving property disputes, their involvement should be approached with sensitivity and respect for their autonomy. It is essential to seek their voluntary participation and honor their decisions and perspectives. In cases where family elders are unable to provide resolutions, seeking professional advice from legal experts or mediators may be necessary.

In conclusion, the role of family elders in resolving property disputes within Indian families is of great significance. Their wisdom, cultural understanding, moral authority, and historical knowledge contribute to the resolution process. By valuing their guidance, seeking their mentorship, and involving them in family discussions, individuals can leverage the unique role of family elders to navigate property disputes effectively, preserve family unity, and foster fair and just outcomes.

Chapter 9. Partition and Division

Explaining the process of partition and division of property

Property disputes in Indian families often necessitate the partition and division of assets as a means of resolving conflicts and ensuring equitable distribution. Partition refers to the legal process of dividing jointly owned property among co-owners or family members with shared ownership rights. It is a complex and multifaceted procedure that requires adherence to legal formalities, consideration of individual rights and entitlements, and the preservation of family relationships. In this chapter, we explore the process of partition and division of property, shedding light on its legal framework, practical considerations, and strategies for navigating this significant aspect of resolving property disputes within Indian families.

Legal Framework: The partition and division of property in India are primarily governed by the Hindu Succession Act, 1956, which outlines the rights and entitlements of family members in joint family property. The act recognizes the concept of coparcenary, which grants equal rights to male heirs in ancestral property. However, subsequent amendments have expanded the scope of inheritance rights to include female heirs as well. Other personal laws, such as the Muslim Personal Law or the Indian Succession Act, may apply to specific communities or situations.

Types of Property Subject to Partition: Partition can apply to different types of property, including ancestral property, self-acquired property, or jointly owned property. Ancestral property refers to property that is inherited up to four generations and remains undivided. Self-acquired property is property acquired by an individual through their own efforts or inheritance. Jointly owned property includes property owned jointly by family members, such as through co-purchasing or inheritance.

Initiating the Partition Process: Partition can be initiated by any co-owner or family member with a legal entitlement to the property. The process begins with the filing of a partition suit or a partition deed, depending on the circumstances and the willingness of family members to cooperate. A partition suit is a legal proceeding filed in court, while a partition deed is a mutual agreement among family members specifying the terms and conditions of the partition.

Identifying and Valuing the Assets: The first step in the partition process is to identify and categorize the assets that are subject to division. This includes conducting a comprehensive inventory of the property, taking into account land, buildings, movable assets, financial assets, and any other relevant assets. It is crucial to obtain accurate valuations of the assets to ensure a fair division and avoid disputes related to undervaluation or overvaluation.

Determining Ownership Shares: The next step is to determine the ownership shares or entitlements of each co-owner or family member. This is based on legal rights, personal contributions, and any existing agreements or understandings among family members. Ownership shares can be determined through legal advice, discussions among family members, or through the intervention of a court-appointed commissioner or valuer.

Establishing the Mode of Division: Once the ownership shares are determined, the mode of division needs to be established. There are different methods of division, including physical division, where the property is physically divided among co-owners, and non-physical division, where the property is divided based on its value. Physical division may not always be feasible or practical, especially in the case of immovable properties, and may require the consent of all co-owners.

Settling Disputed Claims: During the partition process, disputed claims or conflicting interests may arise among family members. It is essential to address these disputes through negotiation, mediation, or, if necessary, through the intervention of the court. Resolving disputed claims is crucial for ensuring a smooth and fair partition process and preserving family relationships.

Partition Deed or Family Settlement: If all family members are willing to cooperate, a partition deed or family settlement can be executed. A partition deed is a legal document that outlines the terms and conditions of the partition, including the division of assets, rights, and responsibilities of each family member, and any other relevant provisions. A family settlement is a mutually agreed-upon arrangement among family members, often facilitated by a mediator or legal advisor, to resolve disputes and divide property amicably.

Legal Proceedings and Court Intervention: In situations where family members are unable to reach an agreement or when disputes cannot be resolved through negotiation, legal proceedings may be initiated. This involves filing a partition suit in court, presenting evidence, and seeking a court-ordered partition and division of the property. Court intervention provides a structured and legally binding resolution process but may also be time-consuming and adversarial.

Tax Implications: Partition and division of property can have tax implications, including capital gains tax, stamp duty, and registration fees. It is important to consult tax advisors or legal experts to understand and comply with the tax regulations associated with the partition and transfer of property. Proper tax planning ensures compliance with legal requirements and minimizes potential tax liabilities.

Adhering to Legal Procedures: Throughout the partition process, it is crucial to adhere to legal procedures and comply with the requirements set forth by the applicable laws. This includes following the prescribed timelines, filing necessary documents, and fulfilling legal formalities such as registration and stamp duty payment. Failure to comply with legal procedures can lead to disputes and complications in the future.

Preserving Family Relationships: The partition and division process can be emotionally challenging and may strain family relationships. It is important to prioritize open communication, empathy, and understanding during this process. Maintaining respect for individual rights, acknowledging the emotional aspects of property division, and seeking the guidance of family elders can contribute to preserving family bonds and fostering a sense of unity.

In conclusion, the partition and division of property are integral aspects of resolving property disputes within Indian families. Understanding the legal framework, initiating the partition process, determining ownership shares, settling disputed claims, and adhering to legal procedures are essential steps in navigating this complex procedure. By approaching partition with transparency, fairness, and consideration for family dynamics, individuals can work towards a resolution that upholds individual rights, preserves family relationships, and ensures the equitable distribution of property.

Chapter 10. Negotiation Techniques

Effective negotiation strategies for reaching fair property settlements

Negotiation is a crucial skill in resolving property disputes within Indian families. It involves engaging in constructive discussions, finding common ground, and reaching mutually acceptable agreements regarding the division and settlement of property. Effective negotiation techniques empower individuals to navigate conflicts, preserve relationships, and achieve fair outcomes. In this chapter, we explore various negotiation strategies that can be employed to resolve property disputes in Indian families, taking into account the legal, cultural, and emotional dimensions involved.

Establishing Common Interests: Successful negotiations often begin by identifying and establishing common interests among the parties involved. This involves finding shared goals, values, and aspirations related to the property dispute. By focusing on common interests, such as financial security, family harmony, or the preservation of shared heritage, individuals can work towards solutions that address the needs and concerns of all parties involved.

Active Listening and Empathy: Active listening is a fundamental component of effective negotiation. It involves attentively hearing and understanding the perspectives, interests, and emotions of the other parties. By actively listening, individuals demonstrate empathy, validate the concerns of others, and create an environment conducive to open communication and trust-building. Practicing empathy helps build rapport, fosters understanding, and paves the way for collaborative problem-solving.

Framing the Negotiation: Framing the negotiation involves setting the tone, defining the issues at hand, and establishing the framework for discussion. It is essential to frame the negotiation in a manner that promotes fairness, transparency, and the preservation of relationships. By emphasizing the importance of a win-win outcome and encouraging cooperative problem-solving, individuals can create an environment where both parties feel heard and valued.

Exploring Interests and Priorities: To reach a fair settlement, it is important to delve beyond positions and uncover the underlying interests and priorities of all parties involved. Interests may include financial security, emotional attachment, or the desire for family unity. By understanding these interests, individuals can identify creative solutions that address the needs and priorities of all stakeholders, leading to more satisfactory outcomes.

Building Trust and Rapport: Trust is a vital component of successful negotiations. Building trust involves demonstrating integrity, transparency, and reliability throughout the negotiation process. By maintaining open lines of communication, being true to commitments, and showing respect for the perspectives of others, individuals can foster trust and rapport, creating a foundation for constructive dialogue and problem-solving.

Generating Options: The negotiation process should encourage the generation of multiple options or alternatives for resolving the property dispute. This requires brainstorming and exploring various possibilities that meet the interests of all parties involved. By expanding the range of options, individuals increase the likelihood of finding creative and mutually satisfactory solutions that go beyond conventional approaches.

Assessing and Evaluating Options: Once options have been generated, it is important to assess and evaluate them objectively. This involves considering the feasibility, practicality, and potential consequences of each option. Individuals should assess the advantages and disadvantages of each proposal and analyze how well they align with the interests and priorities of all parties involved. By conducting a thorough evaluation, individuals can make informed decisions and select options that have the highest chances of success.

Compromise and Flexibility: Negotiation often requires compromise and flexibility from all parties involved. It involves recognizing that achieving a fair settlement may require giving up certain individual preferences or making concessions. By demonstrating a willingness to find middle ground and explore mutually acceptable solutions, individuals create an atmosphere of collaboration and increase the likelihood of reaching a resolution.

Seeking Mediation: In situations where negotiations reach an impasse or become overly contentious, seeking the assistance of a trained mediator can be beneficial. Mediators are neutral third parties who can help facilitate constructive dialogue, manage conflicts, and guide the negotiation process towards a resolution. Their expertise in communication and dispute resolution techniques can help parties overcome barriers and find common ground.

Keeping Emotions in Check: Property disputes can evoke strong emotions, making it essential to manage emotions effectively during negotiations. Emotional intelligence plays a crucial role in maintaining composure, controlling impulses, and focusing on the issues at hand. By recognizing and managing emotions constructively, individuals can approach negotiations with a clear and rational mindset, promoting productive dialogue and problem-solving.

Seeking Legal Advice: While negotiation is often the preferred method of resolving property disputes, it is important to seek legal advice to ensure compliance with applicable laws and protect individual rights. Legal professionals can provide guidance on legal rights, obligations, and potential consequences of different negotiation outcomes. Their expertise contributes to informed decision-making and safeguards the legal aspects of the property settlement.

Documenting Agreements: Once a settlement has been reached, it is crucial to document the agreement in writing. This may involve preparing a legally binding agreement or consent terms that clearly outline the terms of the settlement, the division of property, and any other relevant provisions. Documenting the agreement helps prevent misunderstandings, ensures accountability, and provides a reference for future compliance.

In conclusion, effective negotiation techniques are vital in reaching fair property settlements within Indian families. By employing strategies such as establishing common interests, active listening, empathy, and creative problem-solving, individuals can navigate property disputes with greater success. Building trust, generating options, assessing alternatives, and maintaining flexibility contribute to finding mutually acceptable solutions. Seeking the assistance of mediators or legal professionals when necessary ensures a balanced and legally sound resolution. Through effective negotiation, individuals can resolve property disputes while preserving relationships, promoting fairness, and fostering a sense of unity within the family.

Chapter 11. Mediation

Exploring the role of mediation in resolving property disputes within families

Property disputes within Indian families can be complex and emotionally charged, often straining relationships and causing significant distress. In such situations, mediation emerges as a valuable approach to resolving conflicts. Mediation is a voluntary and confidential process facilitated by a neutral third party, the mediator, who assists family members in reaching a mutually agreeable resolution. This chapter explores the role of mediation in resolving property disputes within Indian families, highlighting its benefits, principles, and techniques that contribute to effective conflict resolution.

Understanding Mediation: Mediation is a collaborative and non-adversarial process that encourages family members to actively participate in resolving their property disputes. Unlike traditional legal proceedings, mediation focuses on communication, understanding, and finding common ground rather than on imposing judgments or decisions. It provides a safe and structured environment for family members to express their concerns, listen to one another, and work towards a fair and sustainable resolution.

The Mediator's Role: The mediator plays a pivotal role in facilitating the mediation process. They are trained professionals with expertise in communication, conflict resolution, and negotiation techniques. The mediator remains neutral, impartial, and unbiased, ensuring that all parties have an equal opportunity to be heard. Their role includes guiding the conversation, managing emotions, exploring options, and assisting family members in finding mutually satisfactory solutions.

Voluntary Nature of Mediation: Mediation is a voluntary process that requires the consent and willingness of all parties involved. It is essential for family members to approach mediation with an open mind and a genuine intention to resolve their disputes. The voluntary nature of mediation empowers individuals to actively engage in the process and take ownership of the resolution, fostering a sense of empowerment and promoting long-term satisfaction with the outcome.

Confidentiality and Privacy: Mediation offers a confidential and private setting where family members can freely express their thoughts, concerns, and interests. Confidentiality encourages open communication and ensures that sensitive information shared during the mediation process remains confidential. This confidentiality fosters an environment of trust, enabling family members to address underlying issues honestly and openly.

Facilitating Communication: Effective communication is crucial in resolving property disputes, and mediation provides a platform for improved communication among family members. The mediator facilitates constructive dialogue, ensuring that everyone has an opportunity to express their perspectives and concerns. Through active listening, paraphrasing, and reframing, the mediator helps family members gain a deeper understanding of each other's viewpoints, fostering empathy and empathy and promoting effective problem-solving.

Identifying Interests and Needs: Mediation emphasizes the exploration of underlying interests and needs of all parties involved in the property dispute. Family members are encouraged to articulate their interests beyond their stated positions, enabling the mediator to uncover common ground and potential solutions. By identifying shared interests, mediation seeks to generate options that address the concerns and priorities of each family member, leading to more sustainable and mutually satisfactory outcomes.

Collaborative Problem-Solving: Mediation promotes a collaborative problem-solving approach that encourages family members to work together towards a resolution. The mediator assists in generating and evaluating creative options, encouraging brainstorming, and exploring alternatives. Collaborative problem-solving empowers family members to take ownership of the resolution process, fostering a sense of shared responsibility and promoting long-term family harmony.

Preserving Relationships: One of the significant advantages of mediation is its focus on preserving relationships. Mediation aims to promote understanding, empathy, and open communication, allowing family members to maintain or rebuild their relationships even after the property dispute is resolved. By emphasizing cooperation, respect, and mutual satisfaction, mediation facilitates a more amicable resolution process that reduces the risk of long-term damage to family dynamics.

Culturally Sensitive Approach: Mediation acknowledges and respects the cultural context within which property disputes occur in Indian families. Mediators are trained to be culturally sensitive, recognizing the impact of cultural norms, traditions, and family values on the resolution process. They adapt their techniques and strategies to ensure that mediation aligns with the cultural expectations and preferences of the family, promoting a more effective and culturally appropriate resolution.

Cost and Time Efficiency: Mediation offers a cost and time-efficient alternative to traditional legal proceedings. By engaging in mediation, families can avoid protracted legal battles, extensive court fees, and prolonged emotional stress. Mediation is typically faster than litigation, allowing family members to reach a resolution within a shorter timeframe and move forward with their lives.

Mediation as a Supportive Process: Mediation provides a supportive environment where family members can voice their emotions, concerns, and anxieties related to the property dispute. The mediator helps manage emotions, diffuse tension, and redirect the focus towards constructive problem-solving. Through their expertise in conflict resolution and communication, mediators create a safe space that encourages healing, understanding, and collaboration.

Complementing Legal Remedies: Mediation can be used in conjunction with legal remedies to resolve property disputes. Mediation does not replace the need for legal advice or the protection of legal rights, but it offers an alternative approach that promotes family autonomy and the preservation of relationships. Mediation can be utilized before or during legal proceedings, helping families explore settlement options and potentially reach an agreement outside of the courtroom.

In conclusion, mediation is a valuable tool for resolving property disputes within Indian families. By providing a voluntary, confidential, and collaborative process, mediation empowers family members to actively participate in finding fair and sustainable solutions.

Through effective communication, exploration of interests, and collaborative problem-solving, mediation promotes understanding, preserves relationships, and offers a cost and time-efficient alternative to traditional legal proceedings. Mediation's culturally sensitive approach and emphasis on support contribute to the resolution of property disputes in a manner that aligns with the unique dynamics and cultural context of Indian families.

Chapter 12. Arbitration

Understanding the process and benefits of arbitration in settling property disputes

Property disputes within Indian families can be complex and contentious, requiring a fair and efficient resolution process. Arbitration emerges as an alternative method to litigation, providing parties with a structured and private means of settling their disputes. This chapter explores the process and benefits of arbitration in resolving property disputes within Indian families, shedding light on its key features, advantages, and considerations.

Understanding Arbitration: Arbitration is a voluntary dispute resolution process where parties agree to submit their property dispute to one or more arbitrators. The arbitrator acts as a neutral third party, tasked with listening to both sides of the dispute, evaluating the evidence presented, and rendering a binding decision called an arbitration award. Arbitration allows parties to resolve their disputes outside of the traditional court system, offering flexibility, efficiency, and privacy.

Agreement to Arbitrate: Arbitration requires the parties involved to agree to submit their property dispute to arbitration. This agreement can be reached before or after the dispute arises and is typically outlined in a contract or a separate arbitration agreement. The agreement defines the scope of the arbitration, the number and qualifications of the arbitrators, the applicable rules, and the process for selecting the arbitrators.

Selection of Arbitrators: The selection of arbitrators is a critical aspect of the arbitration process. Parties can choose a single arbitrator or a panel of arbitrators depending on the complexity and significance of the dispute. It is important to select arbitrators who possess relevant expertise, knowledge of property laws, and experience in dispute resolution. The selection of arbitrators should be impartial, ensuring the fairness and integrity of the arbitration proceedings.

Confidentiality: Confidentiality is a significant advantage of arbitration. Unlike court proceedings, arbitration offers a private setting where parties can discuss their dispute without public disclosure. Confidentiality protects sensitive information, trade secrets, and personal matters from becoming public knowledge. This feature can be particularly beneficial in property disputes within Indian families, preserving privacy and minimizing potential damage to family relationships.

Flexibility in Procedural Rules: Arbitration allows parties to tailor the procedural rules to suit their specific needs and preferences. Unlike litigation, which is bound by formal court procedures, arbitration offers flexibility in terms of timelines, evidence presentation, and the examination of witnesses. Parties can agree on the rules and procedures that best accommodate their unique circumstances, ensuring a more efficient and customized resolution process.

Adherence to Principles of Natural Justice: Arbitration adheres to the principles of natural justice, providing parties with an opportunity to present their case, challenge evidence, and be heard. The arbitrator(s) remain impartial and ensure that each party has a fair and equal chance to present their arguments and evidence. This commitment to fairness and due process enhances the credibility and legitimacy of the arbitration process.

Expertise and Efficiency: Arbitration allows parties to select arbitrators with specific expertise relevant to the property dispute at hand. This expertise enables the arbitrators to understand the complexities of property laws, valuation methods, and other technical aspects involved in the dispute. The arbitrators' knowledge and efficiency contribute to a more streamlined resolution process, potentially resulting in quicker decisions and reduced costs.

Finality and Binding Nature: Arbitration awards are final and binding on the parties involved. This means that once an award is rendered, it is enforceable by law and parties are obligated to comply with the decision. The finality of arbitration awards provides certainty and closure, eliminating the potential for prolonged appeals and legal uncertainties.

Enforceability: Arbitration awards are generally enforceable both domestically and internationally under the New York Convention, which facilitates the recognition and enforcement of arbitration awards across different jurisdictions. This enforceability enhances the efficacy of arbitration as a dispute resolution mechanism, ensuring that the parties can rely on the award to secure their rights and interests.

Cost Considerations: Arbitration can be cost-effective compared to litigation, particularly in complex property disputes. While arbitration does involve costs such as arbitrator fees and administrative expenses, it often avoids the lengthy and expensive litigation process. Parties can save on legal fees, court fees, and related expenses, making arbitration a more financially viable option for resolving property disputes.

Preserving Relationships: Arbitration, like mediation, offers the opportunity to preserve relationships between family members. The private nature of arbitration allows for confidential discussions and negotiations that can help maintain family unity and minimize potential damage to interpersonal dynamics. By resolving the dispute through arbitration, parties can potentially safeguard familial bonds and focus on rebuilding trust and cooperation.

Supplementing Mediation or Negotiation: Arbitration can be used in conjunction with mediation or negotiation as part of a step-wise approach to resolving property disputes. If parties are unable to reach a settlement through mediation or negotiation, they can opt for arbitration as the next step. This allows for a progressive resolution process, starting with more collaborative methods and escalating to a binding decision if necessary.

In conclusion, arbitration offers an effective and efficient method for resolving property disputes within Indian families. Its features, including confidentiality, flexibility, expertise, and enforceability, make it an attractive alternative to traditional litigation. By voluntarily agreeing to submit their disputes to arbitration, parties can benefit from a process tailored to their specific needs, potentially saving time, costs, and preserving privacy. The binding nature of arbitration awards ensures finality and provides a solid foundation for moving forward. Whether used as a standalone mechanism or in conjunction with mediation or negotiation, arbitration empowers families to resolve property disputes in a manner that is fair, efficient, and conducive to maintaining familial relationships.

Chapter 13. Alternate Dispute Resolution

Exploring alternative methods like family settlement and conciliation

When it comes to resolving property disputes within Indian families, traditional litigation is not always the most effective or desirable option. The adversarial nature of the court system can further strain relationships and prolong the resolution process. In such cases, alternative dispute resolution (ADR) methods like family settlement and conciliation offer valuable alternatives. This chapter delves into the concept of ADR and explores the benefits and techniques of family settlement and conciliation in the context of resolving property disputes within Indian families.

Understanding Alternate Dispute Resolution (ADR): ADR refers to methods of resolving disputes outside of formal court proceedings. It provides parties with a more collaborative and flexible approach, encouraging open communication, understanding, and voluntary agreement. ADR methods like family settlement and conciliation prioritize family autonomy, preserving relationships, and promoting a cooperative environment for resolving property disputes.

Family Settlement: Family settlement is an ADR method that involves the voluntary agreement and compromise among family members to settle their property disputes. It is a process where family members come together, either independently or with the assistance of mediators or legal professionals, to negotiate and reach a mutually acceptable settlement. Family settlements can be structured as legally binding agreements, outlining the terms of the settlement, property division, and other relevant provisions.

Importance of Communication: Effective communication is a cornerstone of family settlement. It requires family members to engage in open and honest dialogue, expressing their concerns, interests, and aspirations. Through active listening and empathetic understanding, family members can bridge communication gaps, clarify misunderstandings, and work towards common ground. Communication plays a vital role in building trust, fostering collaboration, and identifying mutually satisfactory solutions.

Negotiation and Compromise: Family settlement heavily relies on negotiation and compromise. Parties must be willing to engage in a give-and-take process, considering the interests and needs of all family members involved. Negotiation involves exploring various options, generating creative solutions, and finding middle ground that respects individual rights and addresses the concerns of all parties. By embracing compromise, family members can navigate the complexities of property disputes and find fair and acceptable resolutions.

Legal Guidance: While family settlement is a more informal and flexible process, it is essential to seek legal guidance to ensure compliance with applicable laws and protect individual rights. Legal professionals can provide advice on the legal implications of the settlement, review the proposed agreement, and ensure that it aligns with legal requirements. Legal guidance contributes to informed decision-making, safeguards individual interests, and promotes a fair and legally sound settlement.

Conciliation: Conciliation is another ADR method that focuses on resolving disputes through the assistance of a neutral third party known as a conciliator. The conciliator acts as a facilitator, guiding family members through structured discussions and negotiations. They help parties identify common interests, address concerns, and explore potential solutions. Conciliation aims to foster understanding, repair relationships, and promote cooperative problem-solving.

Role of the Conciliator: The conciliator plays a crucial role in the conciliation process. They are trained professionals with expertise in conflict resolution and communication techniques. The conciliator remains neutral, impartial, and unbiased, ensuring a fair and balanced process. Their role includes creating a supportive and respectful environment, facilitating communication, managing emotions, and guiding family members towards mutually agreeable solutions.

Confidentiality and Privacy: Family settlement and conciliation offer confidentiality and privacy, allowing family members to engage in open discussions without public exposure. This confidentiality creates a safe space where family members can freely express their thoughts, concerns, and emotions. By preserving privacy, family members can address sensitive issues more comfortably, fostering trust and encouraging open communication.

Preserving Relationships: One of the key advantages of ADR methods like family settlement and conciliation is their focus on preserving relationships. These methods prioritize understanding, empathy, and cooperation, allowing family members to maintain or rebuild their relationships even after the property dispute is resolved. By promoting collaboration and mutual respect, family settlement and conciliation create a foundation for long-term family harmony.

Culturally Sensitive Approach: ADR methods like family settlement and conciliation recognize and respect the cultural context within which property disputes occur in Indian families. These methods can be adapted to align with cultural norms, values, and family dynamics. The flexibility of family settlement and the supportive nature of conciliation make them culturally sensitive approaches to resolving property disputes.

Informal and Cost-Effective: Family settlement and conciliation are generally less formal and more cost-effective compared to litigation. These methods allow families to avoid protracted court battles, legal fees, and extensive court proceedings. By opting for family settlement or conciliation, parties can save on time, expenses, and emotional stress, making them more accessible and affordable options for resolving property disputes.

Compliance and Enforcement: Once a family settlement or conciliation agreement is reached, it is crucial to document and formalize the agreement to ensure compliance and enforcement. This may involve preparing a legally binding agreement or consent terms that clearly outline the terms of the settlement, property division, and other relevant provisions. Formalizing the agreement contributes to accountability and provides a reference for future compliance.

In conclusion, alternative dispute resolution methods like family settlement and conciliation offer valuable approaches to resolving property disputes within Indian families. These methods prioritize collaboration, open communication, and the preservation of relationships. By engaging in family settlement or conciliation, parties can maintain control over the resolution process, find mutually agreeable solutions, and potentially avoid the adversarial nature of litigation. The informal and cost-effective nature of these methods, coupled with their cultural sensitivity, make them effective tools for resolving property disputes in a manner that promotes family unity, understanding, and long-term harmony.

Chapter 14. Role of Courts

Discussing the role of courts in property dispute resolution and the litigation process

In resolving property disputes within Indian families, the role of courts is significant. Courts serve as the formal legal institutions where disputes are adjudicated and decisions are rendered. This chapter explores the role of courts in property dispute resolution and the litigation process, highlighting the key aspects, procedures, and considerations involved.

Judicial System in India: The judicial system in India comprises various levels of courts, including district courts, high courts, and the Supreme Court. Each court has its jurisdiction and authority to hear and decide property disputes based on their legal and territorial limits. The judicial system provides a structured and impartial forum for resolving disputes and upholding the rule of law.

Legal Framework: The legal framework surrounding property disputes in India is governed by various laws and acts, including the Transfer of Property Act, the Indian Succession Act, and the Hindu Succession Act, among others. These laws establish the legal principles, rights, and obligations related to property ownership, inheritance, and dispute resolution. Courts interpret and apply these laws in property dispute cases, providing guidance and legal precedents.

Jurisdiction and Venue: Courts have jurisdiction to hear property disputes based on specific factors such as the nature and value of the property, the location of the property, and the parties involved. The appropriate court for a property dispute is determined by the territorial jurisdiction and the hierarchy of courts. Choosing the correct court and venue is crucial for initiating legal proceedings and ensuring that the dispute is heard by the appropriate judicial authority.

Filing a Lawsuit: To initiate the litigation process, the party seeking resolution of the property dispute must file a lawsuit or a plaint before the appropriate court. The plaint outlines the nature of the dispute, the parties involved, and the relief sought. It is essential to draft the plaint accurately, providing all relevant facts and legal grounds to support the claim.

Pleadings and Documentation: Once the lawsuit is filed, the litigation process progresses through a series of pleadings and documentation. These include the written statements, counterclaims, and additional documents submitted by the parties to support their case. Pleadings play a crucial role in defining the scope of the dispute, presenting arguments, and raising legal issues to be decided by the court.

Evidence and Discovery: Evidence plays a central role in property dispute litigation. Parties are required to present documentary evidence, witness statements, expert opinions, and any other relevant materials to support their claims or defenses. Discovery is a process through which parties exchange relevant information and documents to ensure transparency and a fair trial. Courts have the power to order the production of evidence and examine witnesses during trial proceedings.

Court Proceedings and Trial: Once the pleadings and evidence are submitted, the property dispute case proceeds to trial. Trial proceedings involve presenting oral arguments, cross-examining witnesses, and making legal submissions. The court hears the arguments from both sides, evaluates the evidence, and renders a decision based on the facts and applicable laws. The trial process provides an opportunity for parties to present their case, challenge evidence, and seek a favorable outcome.

Judicial Decisions: Courts have the authority to render judgments or orders based on the evidence and legal arguments presented during trial. The judgment outlines the court's decision, the reasons for the decision, and the relief granted or denied. Judicial decisions establish legal precedents that guide future property dispute resolutions and contribute to the development of property laws.

Appeal and Appellate Courts: Parties dissatisfied with the trial court's decision have the right to appeal to higher courts. Appellate courts review the trial court's decision, evaluate the legal issues, and determine if any errors were made. The appellate process provides an opportunity for parties to challenge the decision, present additional arguments, and seek a reversal or modification of the original judgment.

Enforcement of Court Orders: Once a judgment or order is issued, it must be enforced to ensure compliance. Courts have the power to enforce their decisions, including property division, monetary compensation, or any other relief granted. Enforcement mechanisms may include the issuance of writs, attachment of property, or other legal measures to secure compliance with the court's orders.

Legal Representation: Parties involved in property dispute litigation often engage legal professionals to represent their interests and advocate on their behalf. Lawyers play a crucial role in providing legal advice, drafting legal documents, presenting arguments, and navigating the complex legal process. Legal representation ensures that parties' rights are protected, legal requirements are met, and effective advocacy is conducted before the courts.

Limitations and Considerations: While courts offer a formal and authoritative mechanism for resolving property disputes, there are certain limitations and considerations to keep in mind. Litigation can be time-consuming, expensive, and emotionally taxing. The adversarial nature of the court process can strain relationships and potentially exacerbate conflicts. Additionally, court decisions are binding, leaving parties with limited control over the outcome.

In conclusion, courts play a crucial role in property dispute resolution within Indian families. They provide a formal and structured forum for parties to present their case, present evidence, and seek a legal resolution. The litigation process involves filing a lawsuit, presenting pleadings and evidence, trial proceedings, and the rendering of judgments. While courts offer a mechanism for resolving disputes, it is essential to consider the limitations and associated costs. Parties may need to weigh the benefits and drawbacks of litigation against alternative dispute resolution methods to determine the most suitable approach for their property disputes.

Chapter 15. Legal Remedies

Examining the legal options available for resolving property disputes

Property disputes within Indian families can be complex and emotionally charged, requiring careful consideration of the available legal remedies. This chapter explores the various legal options for resolving property disputes, shedding light on the key principles, procedures, and considerations involved in seeking legal remedies within the Indian legal system.

Legal Framework: Property disputes in Indian families are governed by a comprehensive legal framework that includes various acts and laws. These may include the Transfer of Property Act, the Indian Succession Act, the Hindu Succession Act, and other relevant legislation. Understanding the legal framework is crucial for navigating property disputes and determining the appropriate legal remedies available.

Rights and Entitlements: Before exploring legal remedies, it is essential to understand the rights and entitlements of the parties involved. Different types of property, such as ancestral property, self-acquired property, and joint property, may be subject to different legal principles and rules. Identifying and assessing the rights and entitlements of each party is a vital step in determining the most appropriate legal recourse.

Mediation and Negotiation: Mediation and negotiation, though not strictly legal remedies, are often the first steps in resolving property disputes. These methods involve facilitated discussions, where parties attempt to reach a mutually agreeable settlement with the help of a neutral third party. Mediation and negotiation can be effective in preserving relationships and avoiding protracted legal battles.

Legal Notice: When informal resolution attempts fail, parties may consider issuing a legal notice to the opposing party. A legal notice serves as a formal communication, outlining the grievances, legal claims, and demand for resolution. It acts as a precursor to initiating legal proceedings and signals the intention to pursue legal remedies if the dispute remains unresolved.

Civil Lawsuit: A civil lawsuit is a formal legal action initiated by one party against another in a court of law. In property disputes, parties may file a civil lawsuit seeking remedies such as declaration of title, partition of property, specific performance, or injunctions. Civil lawsuits involve the presentation of evidence, legal arguments, and adherence to procedural rules of the court.

Partition Suit: In cases involving joint ownership of property, a partition suit may be an appropriate legal remedy. A partition suit seeks to divide the property among the co-owners based on their respective shares and interests. The court determines the division of the property and may order its physical division or a monetary settlement based on the circumstances of the case.

Injunctions: Injunctions are court orders that prevent a party from engaging in certain actions or require them to perform specific actions. In property disputes, parties may seek injunctions to prevent the sale, transfer, or alteration of the property until the dispute is resolved. Injunctions can provide temporary relief and maintain the status quo during the legal proceedings.

Specific Performance: Specific performance is a legal remedy that compels a party to fulfill their contractual obligations. In property disputes, specific performance may be sought when one party fails to transfer or convey the property as agreed upon in a contract. If the court finds that specific performance is warranted, it can order the defaulting party to complete the transaction as specified.

Declaration of Title: In cases where there is a dispute regarding the ownership or title of the property, parties may seek a declaration of title from the court. A declaration of title establishes the legal ownership and rights of the parties involved. This remedy is particularly useful when there are conflicting claims or uncertainties regarding the ownership of the property.

Adverse Possession: Adverse possession is a legal principle that allows a person to claim ownership of a property through continuous and uninterrupted possession for a specified period, typically prescribed by law. In certain circumstances, parties may assert adverse possession as a legal remedy to establish their ownership rights over disputed property.

Appeals: If dissatisfied with the decision of the trial court, parties have the right to appeal to higher courts. Appeals provide an opportunity to challenge legal errors, factual findings, or the interpretation of the law. Appellate courts review the trial court's decision and may uphold, modify, or reverse the judgment based on their assessment of the case.

Execution of Judgments: Once a judgment is obtained, parties must ensure its execution. Execution involves the enforcement of the court's order, such as the transfer of property, payment of compensation, or compliance with other directives. Parties can seek the assistance of court-appointed officials, such as a court-appointed receiver or an execution officer, to ensure the execution of judgments.

Limitations and Considerations: It is important to note that legal remedies have certain limitations and considerations. Legal proceedings can be time-consuming, costly, and emotionally challenging. They may strain family relationships and result in unpredictable outcomes. Parties should carefully evaluate the costs and benefits of pursuing legal remedies and consider alternative dispute resolution methods if appropriate.

In conclusion, the Indian legal system offers a range of legal remedies for resolving property disputes within families. Parties involved in property disputes should familiarize themselves with the legal framework, understand their rights and entitlements, and consider the available legal options. Seeking legal remedies involves a strategic approach, balancing the desire for a fair resolution with the potential costs and implications of litigation. Exploring mediation, negotiation, and other alternative dispute resolution methods can also provide valuable avenues for resolving property disputes effectively and preserving family relationships.

Chapter 16. Tax Implications

Understanding the tax implications associated with property division and inheritance

Property division and inheritance can have significant tax implications for individuals involved in property disputes within Indian families. It is crucial to have a clear understanding of the tax considerations and obligations associated with property division and inheritance to ensure compliance with tax laws and to make informed decisions. This chapter explores the key tax implications and provides insights into the tax considerations that arise in the context of resolving property disputes.

Income Tax: Income tax is a direct tax levied on the income earned by individuals. In the context of property division, income tax implications may arise when there is a transfer of property or when the property generates rental income or capital gains. It is important to consider the applicable income tax rules and rates when determining the tax implications of property division.

Capital Gains Tax: Capital gains tax is levied on the profit or gain realized from the sale or transfer of a capital asset, such as land, buildings, or investments. In the case of property division, if there is a transfer of property that results in a capital gain, capital gains tax may be applicable. The tax liability is calculated based on the difference between the sale price and the cost of acquisition or the fair market value of the property.

Inheritance Tax: Inheritance tax is a tax imposed on the value of assets received by individuals through inheritance. In India, there is no specific inheritance tax at the national level. However, some states may levy inheritance tax or estate duty. It is essential to understand the inheritance tax laws applicable in the relevant state and any exemptions or reliefs available.

Gift Tax: Gift tax is a tax levied on the transfer of property without consideration or for inadequate consideration. In the context of property division, if there are transfers of property as gifts, gift tax implications may arise. However, it is important to note that gift tax has been abolished at the national level in India, except for certain cases. Some state governments may impose their own gift tax regulations, and it is important to be aware of the specific state laws.

Stamp Duty and Registration Charges: Stamp duty and registration charges are applicable when transferring or registering property. These charges vary across states and are usually based on the value of the property being transferred. It is crucial to consider stamp duty and registration charges when determining the financial implications of property division and ensuring compliance with the applicable laws.

Wealth Tax: Wealth tax is a tax imposed on the net wealth or assets held by individuals. In India, wealth tax has been abolished at the national level since the assessment year 2016-17. However, it is important to be aware of any state-level wealth tax regulations that may apply.

Exemptions and Deductions: Various exemptions and deductions may be available under the tax laws that can help reduce the tax liability associated with property division and inheritance. These exemptions and deductions may include provisions for the transfer of ancestral property, exemptions for specific types of assets, or deductions for expenses incurred in the transfer process. It is essential to consult with tax professionals or experts to understand and leverage the available exemptions and deductions effectively.

Double Taxation: Double taxation may occur when the same income or asset is subject to tax in multiple jurisdictions. In the case of property disputes involving cross-border assets or parties residing in different countries, it is important to consider the tax implications and potential relief available under double taxation avoidance agreements or treaties.

Tax Planning: Given the complexities of tax implications in property division and inheritance, tax planning plays a crucial role. Effective tax planning strategies can help minimize the tax burden and optimize tax benefits. Engaging tax professionals or experts can provide valuable insights into tax planning opportunities, ensuring compliance with tax laws while maximizing tax efficiency.

Disclosure and Reporting: Proper disclosure and reporting of property transfers, capital gains, and other relevant information to the tax authorities are essential to meet the compliance requirements. Failing to disclose or report taxable transactions accurately can lead to penalties or legal consequences. It is important to maintain accurate records and seek professional advice to ensure proper disclosure and reporting.

Professional Guidance: Given the intricacies of tax laws and the potential impact on property division and inheritance, seeking professional guidance from tax experts or chartered accountants is highly recommended. Tax professionals can provide personalized advice based on individual circumstances, assist in tax planning, ensure compliance with tax laws, and help navigate any complexities that may arise.

In conclusion, understanding the tax implications associated with property division and inheritance is crucial for individuals involved in property disputes within Indian families. Income tax, capital gains tax, inheritance tax, gift tax, stamp duty, and registration charges are among the key tax considerations. Awareness of exemptions, deductions, double taxation provisions, and the importance of tax planning can help individuals make informed decisions and ensure compliance with tax laws. Seeking professional guidance is advisable to navigate the complexities of tax implications effectively and to optimize tax benefits while resolving property disputes.

Chapter 17. Emotional Impact

Addressing the emotional aspects and family dynamics involved in property disputes

Property disputes within Indian families can evoke intense emotions and strain family relationships. These disputes often go beyond the legal and financial aspects, affecting the emotional well-being of the individuals involved. This chapter delves into the emotional impact of property disputes and explores strategies for addressing the emotional aspects and managing family dynamics in the process of resolving such disputes.

Family Dynamics and Interpersonal Relationships: Property disputes can disrupt the dynamics and relationships within a family. Long-standing resentments, misunderstandings, and communication breakdowns may surface during the dispute resolution process. Understanding the unique family dynamics and the underlying issues can help address emotional conflicts effectively.

Emotional Triggers: Property disputes can trigger a range of emotions, such as anger, resentment, jealousy, fear, and sadness. These emotions may arise due to perceived unfairness, a sense of entitlement, or fear of losing valuable assets. Recognizing and acknowledging these emotional triggers is the first step in managing and resolving them constructively.

Open Communication: Open and honest communication is crucial in addressing the emotional impact of property disputes. Encouraging family members to express their concerns, grievances, and perspectives can foster understanding and empathy. Creating a safe space for dialogue allows each person to voice their emotions, facilitating the resolution of underlying emotional conflicts.

Active Listening: Listening attentively and empathetically to family members' viewpoints is essential for effective communication. Active listening involves giving undivided attention, paraphrasing, and validating the feelings and concerns expressed by others. This approach fosters trust, enhances understanding, and promotes a collaborative environment for resolving disputes.

Empathy and Perspective-Taking: Developing empathy and practicing perspective-taking can help individuals understand the emotions and perspectives of others involved in the property dispute. Empathy enables individuals to acknowledge the impact of the dispute on others and promotes compassion and understanding. Perspective-taking allows individuals to view the situation from different angles, facilitating a more comprehensive and inclusive resolution.

Mediation and Counseling: Engaging the services of a professional mediator or counselor can be highly beneficial in addressing the emotional impact of property disputes. Mediators and counselors provide a neutral and supportive environment where family members can openly express their emotions, clarify misunderstandings, and work towards finding mutually agreeable solutions. These professionals can guide the family through the emotional complexities and facilitate effective communication.

Emotional Support: Property disputes can be emotionally draining for individuals involved. Seeking emotional support from trusted friends, family members, or support groups can provide a safe outlet to share feelings and experiences. Emotional support helps individuals cope with the stress and emotional turmoil associated with the dispute, fostering resilience and promoting well-being.

Recognizing Personal Biases: It is essential for individuals to recognize and reflect upon their personal biases and emotional reactions during property disputes. Biases may stem from past experiences, cultural beliefs, or personal insecurities. Acknowledging and addressing these biases allows individuals to approach the dispute with a more objective and rational mindset.

Professional Guidance: In complex property disputes, it may be beneficial to seek professional guidance from therapists, psychologists, or family counselors with expertise in conflict resolution. These professionals can provide guidance on managing emotions, improving communication, and facilitating productive conversations within the family. Their expertise helps create a supportive environment for emotional healing and effective dispute resolution.

Balancing Emotional and Legal Considerations: Resolving property disputes requires a delicate balance between emotional considerations and legal obligations. While addressing emotions is crucial, it is important to ensure that legal rights and obligations are also respected. Engaging legal professionals who specialize in family law can help individuals navigate the legal complexities while addressing the emotional impact of the dispute.

Long-Term Relationship Preservation: Property disputes have the potential to strain long-standing relationships within the family. It is important to prioritize long-term relationship preservation by fostering understanding, forgiveness, and reconciliation. Family members should recognize the value of maintaining familial bonds and work towards resolving conflicts in a way that promotes harmony and future well-being.

Healing and Moving Forward: Resolving property disputes is not solely about reaching a settlement but also about healing and moving forward as a family. Healing requires time, patience, and willingness to let go of past grievances. It may involve forgiveness, rebuilding trust, and embracing new dynamics. Working towards a shared vision for the future can help families move beyond the dispute and rebuild their relationships.

In conclusion, property disputes within Indian families have a significant emotional impact that goes beyond the legal and financial aspects. Recognizing and addressing the emotional aspects of these disputes is crucial for effective resolution and long-term relationship preservation. Open communication, active listening, empathy, and professional guidance play vital roles in managing the emotional impact and facilitating constructive discussions. By embracing understanding, empathy, and healing, families can move forward, rebuilding their relationships and creating a harmonious future.

Chapter 18. Future Planning

Advice on proactive measures for preventing property disputes in the future

Property disputes within Indian families can be emotionally and financially draining, causing significant rifts among family members. While resolving ongoing property disputes is crucial, it is equally important to take proactive measures to prevent such disputes from arising in the future. This chapter offers valuable advice and strategies for future planning to minimize the likelihood of property disputes within Indian families.

Clear and Transparent Communication: Effective communication is the foundation of preventing property disputes. Encouraging open and transparent communication among family members fosters understanding, resolves misunderstandings, and promotes a culture of trust. Regular family meetings or discussions can provide an opportunity to address property-related matters, clarify expectations, and ensure everyone's voices are heard.

Drafting Clear and Comprehensive Wills: Creating clear and comprehensive wills is essential to avoid ambiguity and potential conflicts over inheritance. Engaging the services of a qualified legal professional can help draft wills that clearly outline the distribution of assets, specify beneficiaries, and address any unique family circumstances. Regularly reviewing and updating wills as circumstances change is crucial to ensure their relevance and effectiveness.

Seeking Professional Advice: Engaging professional advice from lawyers, accountants, or financial planners can provide valuable insights and expertise in property and estate planning. These professionals can help navigate legal complexities, provide guidance on tax implications, and develop tailored strategies to protect family assets. Seeking professional advice ensures that the family's interests are safeguarded and future disputes are minimized.

Establishing a Family Constitution: A family constitution is a written document that outlines the principles, values, and guidelines for managing family assets and resolving disputes. Developing a family constitution encourages shared decision-making, defines roles and responsibilities, and sets clear expectations for all family members. It serves as a reference point for future generations, ensuring continuity and preventing conflicts.

Educating the Next Generation: Educating the next generation about property ownership, management, and the importance of family harmony is crucial for preventing future disputes. Inculcating financial literacy, teaching responsible asset management, and fostering a sense of shared responsibility can help the younger generation understand and appreciate the family's wealth and its significance. This education can lay the groundwork for a smooth transfer of assets and reduce the likelihood of disputes in the future.

Creating Trusts and Family Foundations: Establishing trusts or family foundations can provide a structured framework for managing family assets and ensuring their preservation for future generations. These legal structures can facilitate asset protection, enable efficient succession planning, and minimize potential disputes. Consulting legal professionals and financial advisors can help determine the most suitable trust or foundation structure based on the family's specific circumstances.

Fair Distribution of Assets: Fair distribution of assets is essential for maintaining family harmony. Ensuring that assets are divided equitably and in accordance with the wishes of the family members can help prevent resentment and disputes. It is important to consider the needs, contributions, and aspirations of each family member when determining the distribution of assets.

Pre-nuptial and Post-nuptial Agreements: Pre-nuptial and post-nuptial agreements can be useful tools in managing property-related expectations and protecting assets in the event of marriage breakdowns. These legal agreements define the rights and obligations of each spouse concerning property ownership and division. Creating such agreements can provide clarity, protect family assets, and minimize potential disputes in the future.

Documenting Financial Transactions: Maintaining accurate records and documentation of financial transactions related to property acquisitions, transfers, or investments is crucial. This documentation serves as evidence and can help prevent disputes arising from misunderstandings or conflicting claims. Keeping organized records and storing them securely ensures easy access and reference when needed.

Regular Property Evaluations: Periodically evaluating the value of properties and investments can help ensure a fair and up-to-date assessment of assets. This prevents disputes arising from inaccurate or outdated valuations and allows for informed decision-making. Engaging professional valuers or property assessors can provide reliable and unbiased assessments of the family's assets.

Preparing for Contingencies: Anticipating and preparing for contingencies can help minimize potential disputes. This includes planning for unforeseen events such as incapacitation, divorce, or the death of a family member. Having appropriate legal documents, such as power of attorney, health care directives, and succession plans, in place can ensure smooth asset management and reduce the risk of conflicts.

Mediation and Conflict Resolution: In the event of disagreements or conflicts, utilizing mediation and conflict resolution techniques can help prevent disputes from escalating into full-fledged property disputes. Mediators, counselors, or trusted family advisors can facilitate constructive discussions, encourage compromise, and help find mutually acceptable solutions. Timely intervention can prevent misunderstandings from festering and maintain family harmony.

Regular Reviews and Updates: Regularly reviewing and updating property-related documents, such as wills, trust deeds, or family constitutions, is essential to ensure their continued relevance and effectiveness. Changes in family circumstances, legal requirements, or financial situations may necessitate modifications to these documents. Regular reviews and updates reflect the evolving needs and aspirations of the family and prevent potential conflicts arising from outdated provisions.

Fostering a Culture of Collaboration and Harmony: Creating a culture of collaboration, respect, and harmony within the family is key to preventing property disputes. Encouraging cooperation, celebrating shared achievements, and nurturing a sense of collective identity strengthens family bonds and reduces the likelihood of conflicts. Encouraging family members to contribute to decision-making processes and fostering an environment of inclusivity can further promote harmony and prevent disputes.

In conclusion, taking proactive measures and adopting a future planning mindset is crucial for preventing property disputes within Indian families. Clear communication, professional advice, comprehensive estate planning, and a focus on family harmony are essential components of effective future planning. By implementing these strategies and fostering a culture of collaboration, families can mitigate the risk of future disputes and preserve their assets for generations to come.

"Resolving Property Disputes in Indian Families" is a comprehensive guide that navigates the intricate terrain of property conflicts within Indian households. With a deep understanding of the cultural, legal, and emotional aspects, this book equips readers with essential knowledge and practical strategies to address property disputes effectively.

From exploring the complexities of property disputes and their cultural context to differentiating between types of property and understanding the principles of inheritance, each chapter offers valuable insights. Whether it's navigating joint family setups, utilizing the wisdom of family elders, or exploring alternative dispute resolution methods, this book provides a holistic approach to resolving property conflicts.

Additionally, it delves into the legal framework, tax implications, emotional impact, and future planning, ensuring a comprehensive understanding of the subject matter. With its compassionate and informative content, this book aims to empower individuals, families, and professionals in achieving fair and harmonious resolutions for property disputes in the Indian context.

ABOUT THE AUTHOR

Mr. C. P. Kumar is a retired Scientist 'G' from National Institute of Hydrology, Roorkee, Uttarakhand, India. He is also a Reiki Healer and Chakra Balancing practitioner (with pendulum dowsing) and offers Emotional Freedom Technique (EFT) to help individuals with emotional issues. Mr. Kumar has authored many books on technical, spiritual, and social topics.

For further details, you may visit his webpage https://www.angelfire.com/nh/cpkumar/virgo.html

www.ingramcontent.com/pod-product-compliance
Lightning Source LLC
LaVergne TN
LVHW022311200926
848481LV00004B/1283
9798223124320